Making Science Work

Forces and Machines

Terry Jennings

Illustrations by
Peter Smith and
Catherine Ward

Belitha Press

First published in the United Kingdom in 1996 by
Belitha Press Ltd, London House, Great Eastern Wharf,
Parkgate Road, London SW11 4NQ
First published 1996 by Cynthia Parzych Publishing Inc, New York
Copyright © 1996 Cynthia Parzych Publishing Inc

Text copyright © 1996 Terry Jennings

Designed by Arcadia Consultants.

Printed and bound in Spain.

British Library Cataloguing in Publication Data for this book
is available from the British Library.

ISBN 1 85561 532 0

Words in **bold** appear in the glossary on page 31.

PHOTO CREDITS
Art Directors Photo Library: 8
Belitha Press Ltd: 6, 21
Benetton Formula Limited: 18
Brookes & Vernons: 24
BSP International Foundations Ltd/Plant Hire Executive: 10
© Robert Frerck, Tony Stone Worldwide Ltd: 25
Grove Europe/Plant Hire Executive: 28
Jennings, Dr Terry: 15
Liebherr-Werk Ehingen Gmbh: 26
Motor Industry Research Association: 19
NASA: 12
Science Photo Library: 13
VME Construction Equipment GB Ltd, photo
by Grahame Miller: 11

Contents

What is force?

Forces are all around us. We call any kind of push or pull a force. A force can make things go. A force can stop things. Forces can stretch, bend and turn things. Some forces are very large. Some are very small. How many times have you used forces today?

A small pushing force

A large pushing force

A twisting force

Pushing and pulling forces

A large pulling force

5

Machines and tools help to make work easier. A hammer is a simple tool. We can use a hammer to knock nails into wood easily.

A bulldozer is a large machine. A bulldozer makes it easier to move earth and rocks. It uses a lot of force. The big **blade** at the front pushes earth and rocks out of the way. The blade can move up and down. It can also tip forwards and backwards.

A hammer is a simple tool.

A bulldozer

There are many other large machines. They all work by making big forces. There are machines that can push and pull. There are machines that lift and turn. Some of these machines are described in this book.

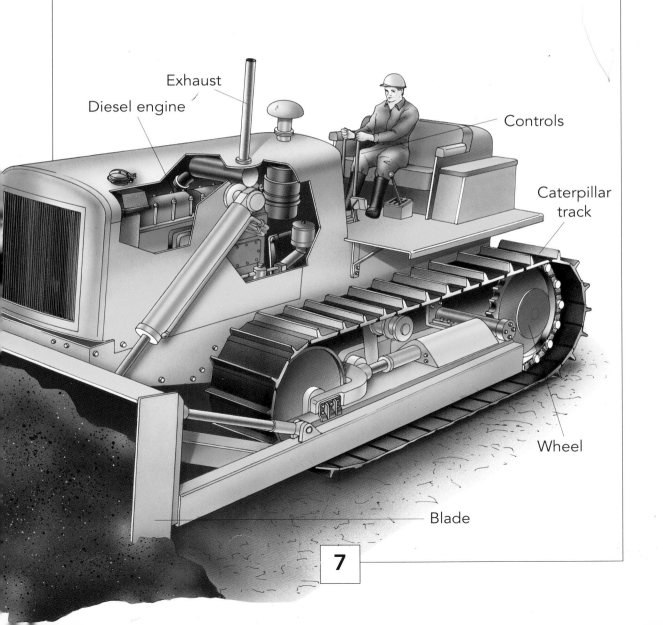

Exhaust

Diesel engine

Controls

Caterpillar track

Wheel

Blade

What happens when you throw a ball up into the air? The ball comes down. This happens because a force pulls things downwards towards the ground. We call this force **gravity**. Gravity pulls on you and gives you weight. It also makes objects fall to the ground. See for yourself.

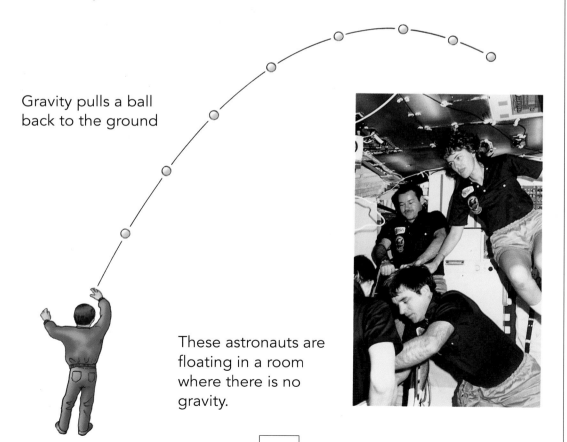

Gravity pulls a ball back to the ground

These astronauts are floating in a room where there is no gravity.

What to do

1 You need a marble, a lighter marble, a metal tray and a chair.

2 Place the tray on the floor. Stand on the chair above the tray.

3 Hold one marble in each hand. Hold your arms up as high as you can.

4 Drop both marbles at the same time. You will see that the heavy marble and the light marble land at the same time. Gravity pulls the two marbles to Earth at the same speed.

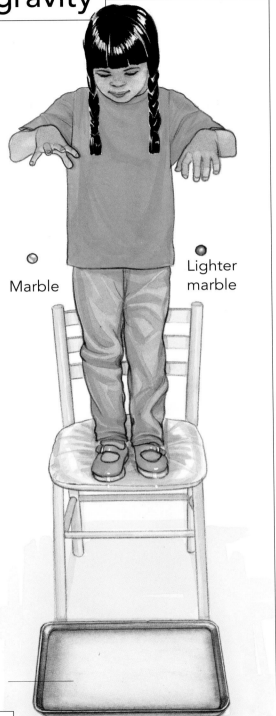

Marble

Lighter marble

Metal tray

A pile driver

G ravity can be useful. A machine called a **pile driver** is used to hit steel posts into the ground. It lifts a heavy object, which falls on the posts because of gravity.

An object on a string always hangs straight down. Gravity pulls the object down. The string and object can be used to check that things are standing up perfectly straight. This is called a plumb line. Builders use a plumb line to check that walls are straight.

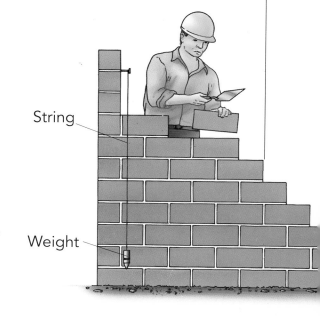

String

Weight

Using a plumb line

Gravity can also help a hammer to knock a nail into wood. Gravity makes water move down a hill. Gravity makes the earth pour out of this dumper truck.

Gravity helps a dumper truck to shed its load.

Because the Earth is so big, gravity at its surface is quite strong. Spacecraft have to push with a force stronger than gravity to get into space. The space shuttle weighs about 2 million kilograms. It has huge rocket engines. Inside the rocket engines, fuel is burned very quickly. Hot gases shoot from the rocket. They push the rocket into space.

The space shuttle *Atlantis* being launched

The Moon is smaller than the Earth. The force of gravity at its surface is not as strong as gravity at the Earth's surface. On the Moon, an astronaut weighs much less than he or she weighs on Earth.

Flight deck

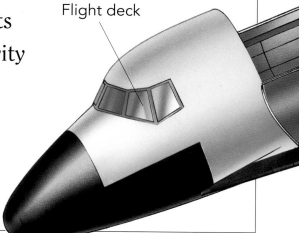

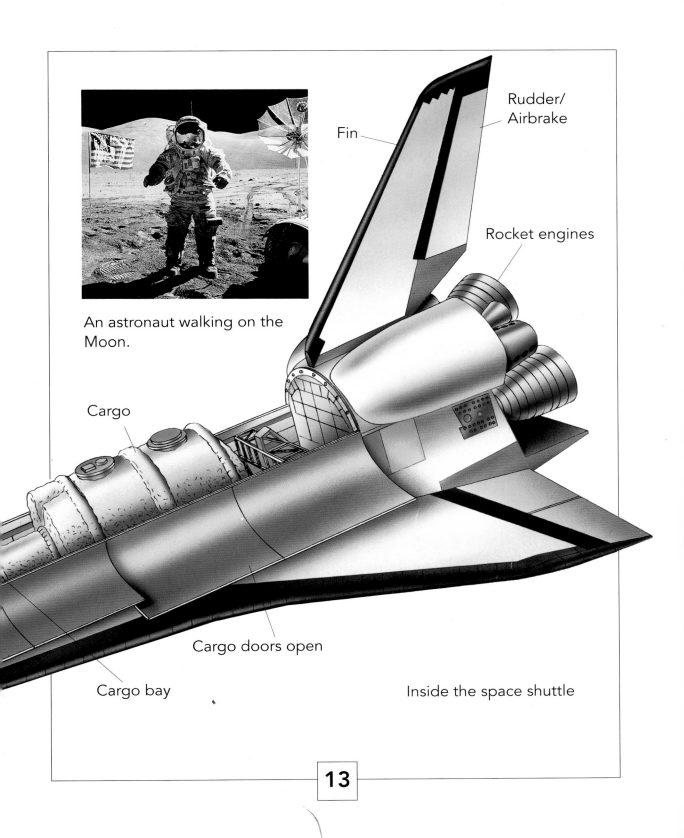

An astronaut walking on the Moon.

Rudder/ Airbrake

Fin

Rocket engines

Cargo

Cargo doors open

Cargo bay

Inside the space shuttle

The force of friction

When you pedal a bicycle, the back wheel turns. This pushes the bike forwards. If you stop pedalling on a flat surface, the bike slows down. This is because the wheels rub against the axle. The wheels slow down because they rub against the road. This rubbing makes a force called **friction**. Friction makes things slow down and stop. You also make friction as you move through the air. This slows you down too.

You can slide on ice because there is hardly any friction. It is not easy to walk or run on ice though. You need friction for your shoes to hold on to the ground.

Many machines have moving parts that rub against each other. This slows the machine down and makes the parts wear out. When oil is put on the moving parts, it makes them slide over each other more easily, by reducing friction.

Oiling a bicycle

The forces used in riding a bicycle

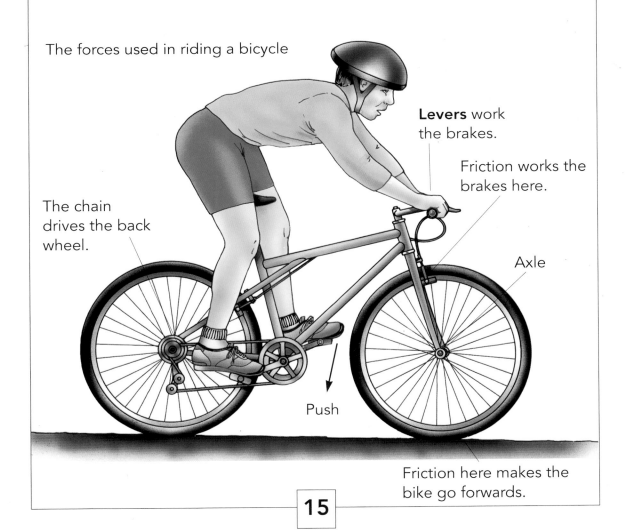

Levers work the brakes.

Friction works the brakes here.

The chain drives the back wheel.

Axle

Push

Friction here makes the bike go forwards.

Testing friction

What to do

1 Find a rubber, a stone, a small piece of wood and an ice cube.

2 Put these objects in a line on a smooth wooden board, about one metre long. Carefully place a book under the end of the wooden board. Which things slide down the board?

3 Now put them back at the end of the wooden board. Place two books under the board. Which things move this time? Do they move more easily? Do they move less easily?

4 Now cover the wooden board with cloth. Repeat the experiment. Which surface makes more friction?

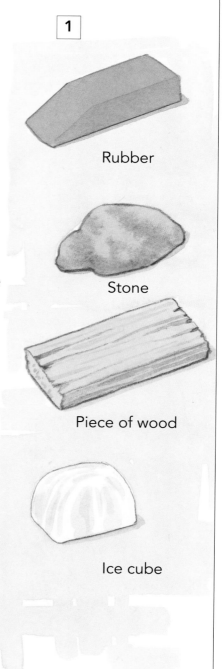

1

Rubber

Stone

Piece of wood

Ice cube

2

One book

Wooden board

3

Two books

4

Cloth

You have to push through the air when you walk, run or ride a bicycle. This causes friction between you and the air. The faster you go, the more air you have to push through. Friction slows you down. Aeroplanes and fast cars are shaped so that the air moves past them easily. Giving something a shape which causes less friction is called **streamlining**.

This racing car is streamlined. It is shaped so that the air flows over it easily. There are no large flat surfaces that stick up and push against the air.

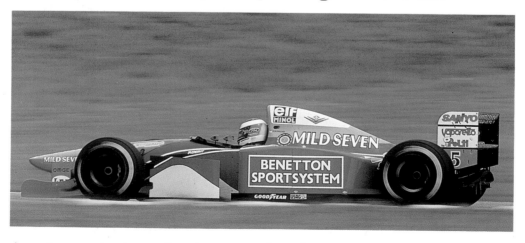

A racing car is streamlined to cause less friction.

Engineers use a wind tunnel to test car shapes. This tells them if the cars are streamlined. Powerful fans make air move past the car. Engineers can see which parts of the car stop the air. Streamlined cars and aeroplanes can go faster. They also use less **fuel**.

Testing a car in a wind tunnel

Levers are **simple machines**. Simple machines make it easier to do work. Levers can change a small force into a large one. Levers can also change the direction of a force. Most levers move things. The thing you want to move is called the **load**. The force of lifting, pulling or turning is called the **effort**. The place where the lever turns is called the **fulcrum**.

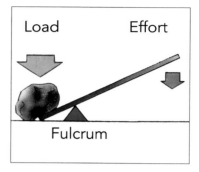

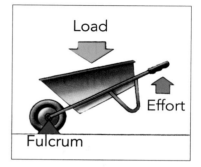

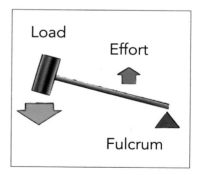

There are three main types of levers.

Many of the things you use every day are levers. You can use a screwdriver to lift the lid off a paint tin. The screwdriver is used as a lever. A door, scissors and a hammer are also levers.

Using a hammer to remove a nail

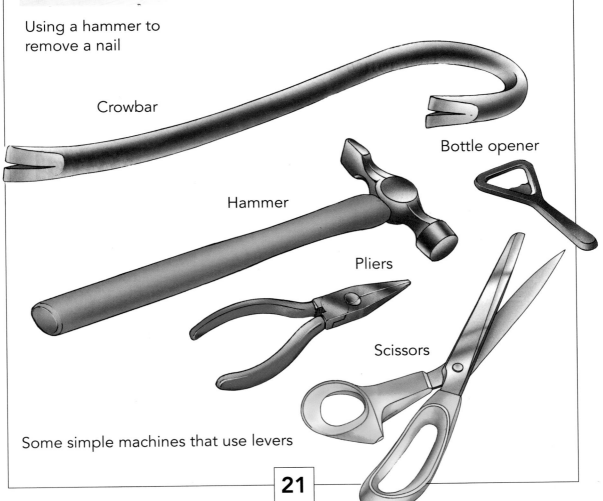

Crowbar

Bottle opener

Hammer

Pliers

Scissors

Some simple machines that use levers

21

What to do

1 Choose a heavy book. Lift it and feel how heavy it is. Now make a lever. **Balance** a 30 cm ruler across a pencil to do this. Rest the book (the load) on the first 3 cm of the ruler. Slide the pencil (the fulcrum) under the 20 cm mark of the ruler.
2 Use one finger to press down on the end of the ruler (the effort).

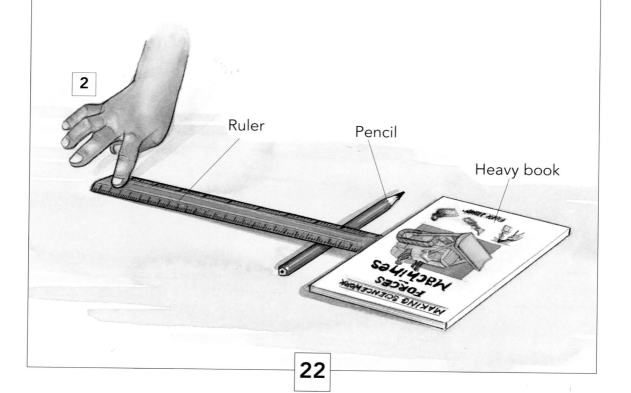

Ruler

Pencil

Heavy book

3 Now move the pencil to the 10 cm mark on the ruler. Press down on the end of the ruler with the same finger. Is it easier or harder to lift the book now? Levers lift things most easily when the fulcrum is as close to the load end as possible.

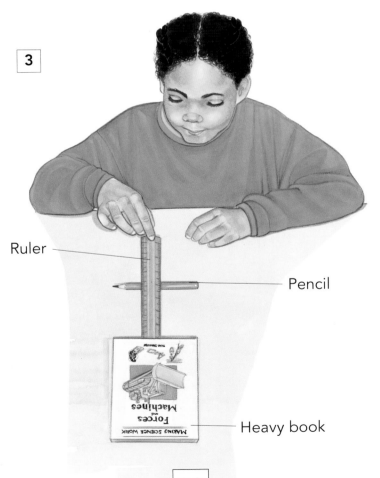

3

Ruler

Pencil

Heavy book

Many large machines use levers. Diggers are machines that dig holes. The digger is made in two parts. These are called the boom and the arm. The boom, the arm and the bucket are all levers.

A digger being used to dig a hole.

The platform of a fire engine works like a digger. The boom is made in two parts. Each of these parts is a lever. The platform where the fire fighters stand is also a lever. This platform can lift fire fighters high above the ground. They can then fight fires and rescue people from tall buildings.

The platform where the fire fighters stand is a lever.

Like levers, **pulleys** also make it easier to lift things. A pulley is a grooved wheel with a rope, a chain or a **cable** over it. The end is tied to something heavy. Using just one pulley, you can lift a load upwards, by pulling the rope downwards. This is easier than lifting the object with no pulley at all. Using two pulleys, it is easier still. You do not need as much effort to lift the load. But you have to pull the rope twice as far.

Pulleys make it easier to lift heavy objects.

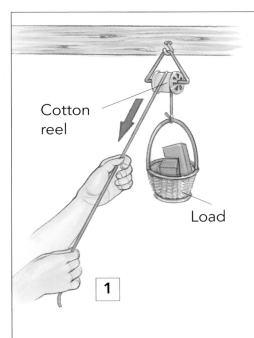

Cotton reel

Load

1

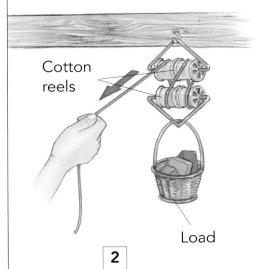

Cotton reels

Load

2

What to do

1 Push some stiff wire through a cotton reel. Bend the ends of the wire into a triangle. Hang the pulley from a hook. Tie one end of some string to an object. Put the string over the pulley. Measure how far you have to pull the string to lift the object 30 cm.

2 Now use two pulleys. You need two cotton reels. Use the same object you used before. How far do you have to pull the string to lift the object 30 cm?

Cranes and lifts

Cranes use pulleys to lift and move heavy loads. This tower crane is used for work on tall buildings. The **counterweight** is made of heavy **concrete** blocks. The counterweight stops the load from pulling the crane over.

This crane can be moved. The counterweight is built into the bottom of the crane. Folding feet keep the crane from falling over.

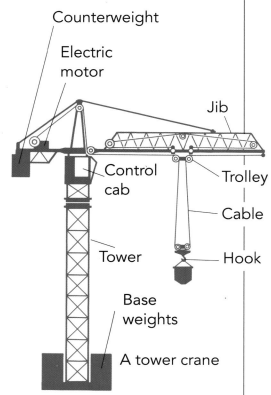

Counterweight

Electric motor

Jib

Control cab

Trolley

Cable

Tower

Hook

Base weights

A tower crane

A mobile crane

A lift has a heavy counterweight. This balances the weight of the car. The lift motor, then, only has to lift the weight of people and goods inside the lift.

Pulley

Motor

Car

Counterweight

A lift

Make your own lift

What to do

1 Push a knitting needle through a cotton reel. Lay a heavy book on the needle.

2 Put a piece of thin string over the cotton reel.

3 Tie a plastic cup of sand on the end of the string. This is your counterweight.

4 Tie a small box to the other end of the string. This is your lift car.

5 Put modelling clay in the box. Does your lift move down? Take some of the clay out of the box. Does the lift go up?

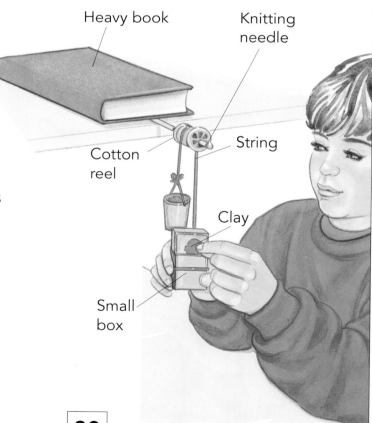

Heavy book

Knitting needle

Cotton reel

String

Clay

Small box

Glossary

Balance To keep or make something steady; to share weight equally on both sides of something.

Blade The wide, flat part of something such as a shovel or a bulldozer.

Cable A strong rope or wire.

Concrete A material made of cement, sand, and water.

Counterweight A weight used to balance something heavy, so that the weight can be moved easily.

Crane A large machine with a long arm. The arm can move up and down and left and right. Cranes are used to lift and carry heavy objects.

Effort The force needed to do work.

Force Any kind of pushing or pulling.

Friction The force that slows down moving objects; the drag when two surfaces are rubbed together.

Fuel Anything that is burned to make heat energy such as coal, gas, oil, or wood.

Fulcrum The point at which a lever turns.

Gravity The force that attracts things towards the Earth.

Lever A simple machine with a bar that turns around a fixed point. Levers are used for lifting weights or forcing something open.

Load The weight moved by a simple machine.

Pile driver A machine for driving down piles, or poles, into the ground.

Pulley A simple machine that has a wheel with a groove in the rim for a rope to run over. It is used to lift things.

Simple machine A machine that has few or no moving parts.

Streamlining Making something, such as an airplane, car, or ship, so that it moves smoothly through the air or water.

Index